Honor Thy Art

How To Be An Extremely Successful Artist

Written by

Barbie The Welder

Cover design by my amazing, creative, kind friend,

Dan Hundycz

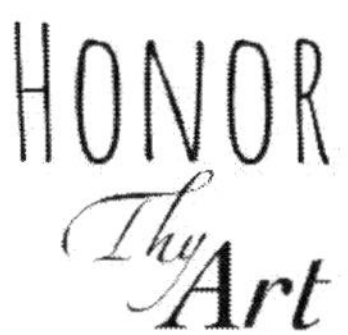

Also written by Barbie The Welder

Horseshoe Crafts; More Than 30 Easy Projects You Can Weld At Home

The Inspiration Blueprint; How To Design & Create Your Inspired Life

How To Weld Silverware Animals; Metal Art Welding Projects

How To Weld Scrap Metal Art; 30 Easy Welding Projects You Can Make At Home

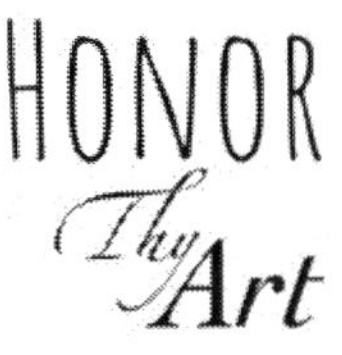

Dedication

I dedicate this book to you, the artist, who has the courage to share your beautiful art with the world, keep that shit up, it's awesome!

With love and gratitude,

Barbie The Welder

HONOR *Thy Art*

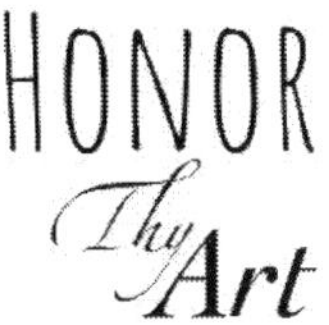

Contents

Forward

"Man Up!"...... "To Be The Man You Gotta Beat The Man"...... "Drop your Cocks and grab your Socks!" Barbie The Welder makes all of these sayings seem Cute! The one saying that stands the truest is "Pull Yourself Up By Your Bootstraps" as Barbie has done just that. From way back in the sticks of rural New York State this young mother decided to provide for herself by following her passion. Learning the art of welding one tool and one piece of equipment at a time while having to figure out how to make it all work in her small shop. With very limited space, drafty and virtually no heat during the brutal New York winters Barbie has managed to build her business along with her unique brand. As Barbie perfected her craft, she started her quest to share her art with the world by loading up her truck, including her son, and heading out to events where she was able to validate that people would appreciate and purchase her creations. Not only was the truck necessary to get the art to the events it also sometimes served as the living quarters for her and her young son. Barely making ends meet and knowing that she had to think bigger Barbie attacked social media and went global with her daily virtual broadcast from her shop. Showing her "works in progress" while also sharing her outlook on life, philosophies and work ethic Barbie has now built up a following of tens of thousands of fans of both her art and her infectious positive personality. Obviously, an inspiration to all women with her ability to stand beside any man with her rod in hand, Barbie is also an inspiration to all artist and art lovers. Barbie stands true to following her dreams and look out when she says" Who Knows What I Will Do Next!" She calls herself" Barbie The Welder" but I call her "Barbie America's Welder"!

Jesse James Dupree

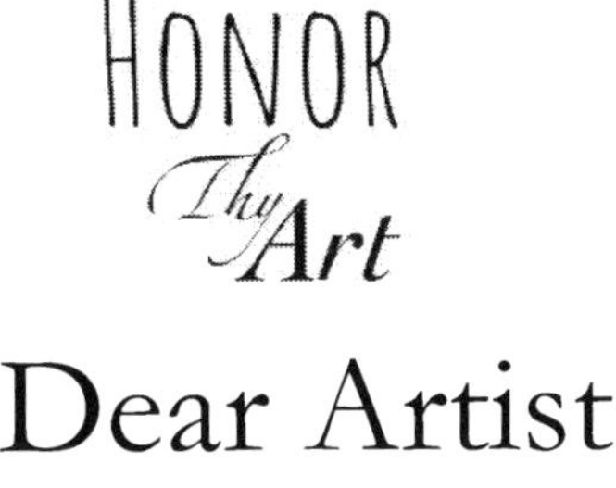

Dear Artist

It's art, anything can happen!

-Barbie The Welder

You are one ballsy SOB and I love that about you! Not every artist will have the courage to say they want to create legacy with their art, but many feel that way, most are just scared what their friends and family will say, they fear judgment. Here's the deal, you're an artist and you deal with judgment every time you produce art, it's literally part of what you do for a living, so let's give them something to really talk about!

By picking up this book you are telling yourself that you and your art want legacy, and I'm here to tell you, you made the right move and I'm so proud of you! You and your art are amazing and unique, and the world needs you both now more than ever! It is your responsibility as a creator to bring your special kind of magic to the masses and there's only one way to do that and that's to play HUGE! No more of this think big crap, the world needs you to think and play HUGE!

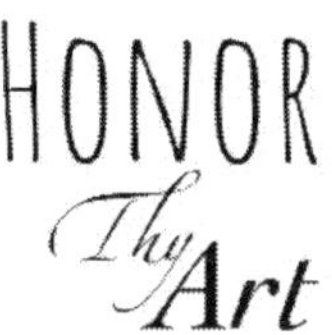

When I started as an artist, I had no idea the possibilities that were out there for an artist. I had no idea the positive self-esteem, happiness, experiences, and financial prosperity that it would bring me. (Do you see the order that is written in? That's the exact order in which my life improved!)

Being happy as an artist is where the success is. It's where your best art is created which will attract clients who are thrilled to pay you and you will attract all sorts of amazing experiences and opportunities into your life! The happiness is what brings everything else, especially the money!

What I've outlined in this book are the exact steps I took to build a worldwide brand, have paying sponsors approach me and want me to work with them, sell my art to major corporations like Harley Davidson, Miller Welders, Carolina Shoe Company, Weiler Abrasives, and Chicago Pneumatic, work with exclusive clients all over the world including rock stars and TV stars.

I've been **paid** to showcase my skills and art at major events all over the United States including creating art live in front of thousands at SEMA in Las Vegas, Sturgis Motorcycle Rally, and Americade Motorcycle Rally. I've written and published 5 books, and thrive financially as an artist creating exactly what I want and working with clients I choose.

Is it possible for you to have similar results? Hell yeah!

Will this happen overnight? Hell NO!

Will it take hard work? Hell yeah!

Will it be worth it? **Absofreakinglutely!**

I guarandamntee that if you put in the work to find your happiness as an artist and stay there long enough the clients with the money and some really incredible opportunities will show up.

Every single chapter in this book is vital for your success. Study, take notes, and do the work! It's going to be challenging, it's going to take time, but I promise if you put in badass effort you WILL GET BADASS RESULTS, and like me, you will be blown away by the clients, art, and opportunities that come into your life!

When you put all the lessons together you will have everything it takes to be a massively successful

ARTREPRENEUR.

(Artist + Entrepreneur= Artrepreneur)

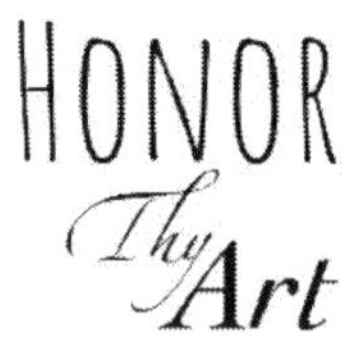

I challenge you to have fun, experiment, and be creative with what I've outlined, **enjoy the process**! You're an artist, it's what you do!

I am so excited to hear from you and experience your art! Email me at BarbieTheWelder@Yahoo.com and show me what you're working on, share your business goals, or tell me about your wins as an artrepreneur!

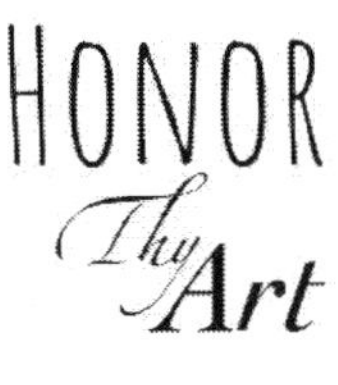

Honor Vision

Success is the result of having a vision so strong that obstacles, failure, and loss only act as motivation.

-Barbie The Welder

The love of creation

Creating your art from love produces your most exquisite work. When I saw the woman creating the giant angel wings in the movie Cast Away, I fell in love with metal art! (I believe in love at first sight!) When I was working as an artist part time in the beginning of my career, I created everything from that place of love. I would have an idea for a sculpture and then I would create it. When I got to the point where I felt like the sculpture could be improved no more, I would take a step back and look at it and would have this amazing moment that is pure with love, gratitude, and pride in craftsmanship. An artist's high. Later, when I was a full time artist, my failure to sell art and provide for my family had me creating from a place of fear. My work was not as good and there was no high when I looked at the sculpture and decided it could be improved no more.

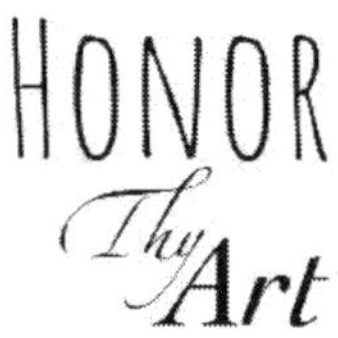

The more I watched my bank account dwindle the more fear my sculptures were being created from and the worse I felt. It was at this point I attended the Erin Woodfest, a show in my hometown of Erin, NY where chainsaw sculptors were creating art live in front of an audience. I was watching them do a speed carving and looked over and saw an artist step back from a piece they were creating and have that pure moment of love, gratitude, and pride in craftsmanship and it changed everything. I started creating art because I knew it was what I was meant to do, not because I wanted to make money. I went back into my studio with the attitude that I don't give a rat's tiny ass if I make money, I was going to create art I love. The weird thing that happened is I started making money. Creating from a place of love allowed me to create my best work yet and people responded by purchasing it. It didn't happen overnight, it took two weeks, but money started coming in!

I know firsthand how insanely scary it can be to be an artist, but I also know firsthand how insanely rewarding it can be. When you learn to work through the fear and work only from love, gratitude, and pride in craftsmanship your world will shift, and you will create yourself an art utopia beyond anything you can ever imagine!

As you work to build your business keep first things first and remember to always create from love, gratitude, and pride in craftsmanship in all that you do but especially in your art!

Does art utopia exist

When you take a road trip you have options, you can hop in the car and head in the direction you want to go hoping you will get where you want to, or you can get directions by using a navigation app on your phone or your vehicles GPS. Both ways will get you there, but one is much more efficient and will allow you to spend maximum time enjoying yourself at your destination.

When it comes to creating a business that serves you, it works the same way. You can throw yourself into making art and just kind of wing it, hoping clients will show up and you'll be able to afford your bills each month, or you can get real damn clear on what your perfect artist life would look like and create a GPS that will take you to your destination as quick as possible, allowing you the freedom to spend your time creating exactly what you want, working with who you want, and making as much money as you want.

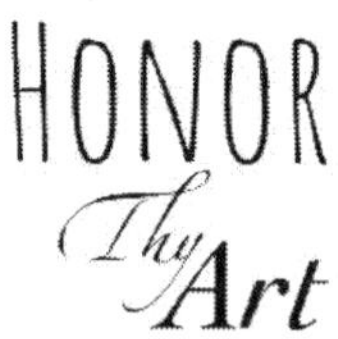

I know you're sitting there right now asking yourself does an art utopia really exist, can I really choose to make what I want for whom I want and make as much as I want, and I'm here to tell you yes, it absolutely does, if you're willing to put in the work to make it happen. It's currently March and if I wanted, I could take the rest of the year off, and all my bills are already paid. When I say take the year off, I truly mean a toes in the water, ass in the sand, freaky umbrella drink in my hand, year off. Will I take the year off? Hell NO! I love what I do every day! I love the challenge of improving my art and my business, it makes my heart sing and feeds my soul. I love, and I mean LOVE the clients I get to work with, and I love what I create for them! I have to be disciplined and schedule days off and force myself not to work! I am the nucleus of a perfect art utopia, and if I can do it **YOU CAN TOO!**

How did I get to this point in my career? I sure didn't start out like this! I spent the first year making art and hoping like hell buyers would show up at my door and buy what I was making. I was making art but other than an occasional post on Facebook I wasn't advertising. I'm not dumb, but damn, girl, how are people supposed to buy something they don't know exists? I was creating art, but I had no idea that I was running a business, so I never thought to study what it took to create a successful business.

I had no direction other than to spend each day creating art with my hand on my ass hoping someone would show up and buy it. (The art, not my ass!)

After a year of working diligently as a starving artist, I got really tired of my dire financial situation and Ramen Noodles for breakfast, lunch, and dinner. (Don't get me wrong I love them, but I want to eat them by choice not out of necessity!) I decided to get a very clear picture of what I wanted my business to look like, what style sculpture I wanted to design and create, how I wanted my business to serve me, what kind of clients I wanted to work with, how much money I wanted to make, and then I asked myself how could I make it all happen. I also grew really thick skin and looked at myself nonjudgmentally and asked myself where I was weak and where could I improve. (The answer was, and still is everywhere.) I got laser focused and spent my time on the things that mattered most, worked to build a solid foundation for my business, and over the next 4 years I created my art utopia.

During those 4 years I worked 14-16 hour days 7 days a week and I made many sacrifices with my time and art but those sacrifices paved the road to artist utopia! I mass produced art that I could make and sell quickly and traveled to craft shows almost every weekend selling my art, and only occasionally was I able to create something that was one of a kind.

Was craft shows my thing? They were at first, they allowed me to pay my bills and let people know I existed as an artist, but mass producing art was not what I wanted to do. I was at the mercy of the people in charge of the events I attended, how much they charged me to set up and sell, advertising of the event or lack thereof, the weather, the people set up next to me, and a slew of other variables, not to mention I slept first in my Jeep and then in my truck at these events because I couldn't afford a hotel. Was I living my vision? NO! Did I want to be mass producing art and sleeping in my truck all up and down the east coast? NO! I was working toward my vision and I was willing to do whatever it took to get to where I am today! I knew that if I worked hard enough, long enough, on the right things that it wasn't a matter of if it was a matter of when I would be living my vision.

Creating a clear vision of your business will give you direction. You will know what areas you need to work on to get you where you want to go as fast as possible. The clearer you are on what you want for yourself, and the more focused you are on doing the work that matters, the faster you will create your art utopia.

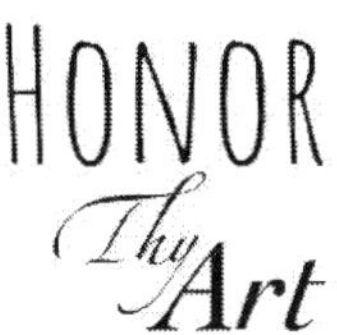

Chances are in the beginning of your career you will have to make sacrifices like I did to create a business that feeds your heart and soul. You may have mass produce art, sing other people's songs, or work a full time job while you build your art business on the side.

Your vision is what will allow you to create a solid foundation for your business, therefore your vision needs to be so freaking exciting that every time you think about it you want to do the happy dance and squeak out a couple tears of joy!

If being an extremely successful artist is deeply important to you, you will do whatever it takes to make it happen. (As long as you are not hurting yourself or anyone else.) I will say this often throughout this book, make this a game, have fun, experiment, be creative, and **enjoy the process**! You're an artist, it's what you do!

Directions To Your Art Utopia

Your art utopia will be different from mine. Creating art in front of thousands of people is my thing but may not be your thing. It's up to you to define your happiness as an artist, your utopia.

We are going to play a game called what does your perfect day as an artist look like! It's quite simple and very fun!

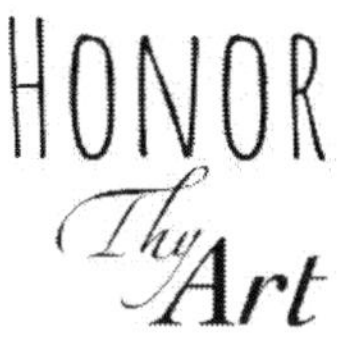

Close your eyes and imagine if you could have the most incredibly perfect day as an artist what would it look like?

Think HUGE! Don't be playing small and limit yourself! We're talking sky's the limit here!

What would your perfect artist day look like?

What art would you create?

What would your studio/shop/work environment look like?

Where would it be?

Are there other artists you want to work with?

Who would they be?

What would it feel like to work with them?

What kind of client would you want to work with? Actors, rock stars, major corporations, little old grandmas? People in your town or city or clients globally?

How would it feel to work with these clients?

How much money do you want to earn in a day, a week, a month, a year?

Write down your answers to the questions so you have a clear picture of what you're working towards. Once you have answered all the questions and know what your vision is make a vision board. Use a giant piece of cardboard or poster board and draw or glue pictures of each piece of your vision on, or print out the words in a cool font, or use a giant whiteboard like I did. However you choose to design your vision board keep it where you will see it every day so that you can make sure you are staying focused on what matters most and growing yourself as an artist and as a business. When you look at your vision board feel what it would feel like to be living in that vision!

However you envision your business it should be feeding your soul and making you happy!

Your vision is destination, your end result desired, but in order to get that end result you will need turn by turn directions. Knowing the steps you need to take to get the destination and setting goals to achieve those steps will give you the turn by turn directions needed to get to your destination.

If you know you want to create paintings live for audiences, you will need to problem solve how to make that happen. You may need to connect with bands who will let you work with them on stage as they preform or create your own live art show and promote it to events.

If you are a singer and want your own record label you will need to problem solve how to do that.

Look at every part of your vision and think about the steps you will need to take to get there. Every step might not show itself to you immediately and will be shown to you as you move forward but your mission is to problem solve as many of the steps as possible and return to this process as many times as necessary until every step reveals itself.

In the beginning my vision was to create one of a kind sculptures I loved, and I figured in order to do that I would need enough passive income to pay my bills so I can take as much time as I wanted to make the sculptures I loved. I didn't know how to make passive income, so it became my mission to figure out how.

Your vision is huge and may seem daunting and unachievable right now but when you break it down into small steps it's much easier to see how you will get to your huge vision and it removes the intimidation factor.

As you grow as an artist your vision will change. Reevaluate your vision at least every 6 months so that your business continues to grow with you and continues to serve you. When your vision changes, update your vision board or create a new one, and then problem solve your steps to get there and set goals to achieve those steps.

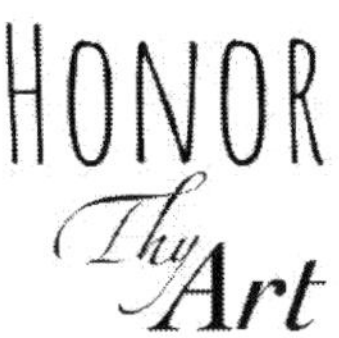

If your vision is not strong then none of this will work. You won't have the motivation to put in the work. When your vision is strong then you will do whatever it takes to make sure that your foundation is strong, no matter how much time it takes. Keep your vision so strong that obstacles, failure, and loss only act as motivation!

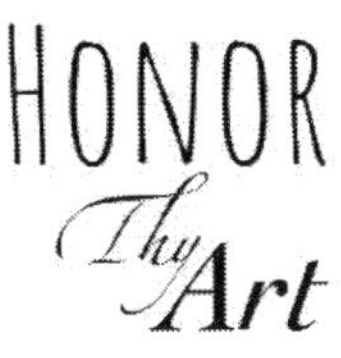

Honor Time

Learning to focus on what matters most and having a long game mentality has helped me be happy and successful as an artist!

-Barbie The Welder

Your time is your most valuable asset and you can't get it back once its past, so doesn't it make the most sense to squeeze every bit of value out of every second that you are capable of? We all get the same 24 hours every day, so how is it that some people are extremely successful, and others just barely squeak by? It all comes down to how they spend their 24 hours.

Now this next part is pretty delicate because as an artist I know how much you deeply love your freedom! I do too! I literally came out of the womb with blue war paint on my face, sword held high, screaming my battle cry of FREEDOM!!! (Think Braveheart!) To my parent's dismay, when I was 5 five years old, I filled my wagon with my underwear and ran away because I felt the constraints of my home were overbearing.

No Shit! Don't worry it only lasted a half hour, I walked around the block but couldn't go any further because I wasn't allowed to cross the street.

I've always valued my freedom above all other things, so this next part was the most challenging for me, being disciplined and scheduling myself. What made it easier was I chose what I scheduled. In the beginning I only scheduled creation time, today, because I've seen the huge benefit of being focused and scheduled, I schedule everything! Every chapter of this book is an area that's sacred to me and scheduling those areas and consistently working at each of them is what has allowed me to grow myself into an extremely successful artist.

Honor Your Schedule

As you read each chapter schedule that area into your daily routine. For each thing you schedule also schedule a reward for accomplishing that thing. Your rewards can be as simple as taking 5 minutes to pet the dog, drinking a cup of your favorite tea, or closing your eyes and imaging receiving a giant trophy for your achievement. However you choose to reward yourself for each success add it to your schedule and make sure you reward yourself every single time you stick to your schedule.

For example:

Monday 7am to 8am study marketing = Reward: Breakfast at my favorite diner

Monday 10am to 5pm create art = Reward: 30 minute bubble bath

Monday 6pm to 6:30pm meditation = Reward: TV for 1 hour

Monday 8pm to 9pm Education video, podcast, or book by a dream chaser = Reward: Favorite snack

Monday 9:30pm to 10:30pm Study branding = Reward: 30 minutes with your favorite pet

We know that over time studying, creating art, meditation, and self-improvement will improve our business, but sometimes it's hard to see the long term rewards. By scheduling rewards you love for each activity, you get instant gratification and will be much more likely to keep your schedule and stay disciplined, therefore you will see incredible results quicker!

Sometimes life happens and you won't be able to keep your schedule. DON'T BEAT YOURSELF UP! No harsh judgment, no negativity, just get back on track and back to rewarding yourself as soon as possible.

Where do I spend my time?

I set Mondays aside for interviews, phone calls, conferences, speaking engagements, and anything else I need to do in regard to my business that doesn't involve creation. I also study a dream chaser, learn a new artistic skill, and meditate.

Tuesday-Sundays I have time scheduled for creation, self-improvement, meditation, studying branding and marketing, social media, and learning a new artistic skill.

Even though I'm extremely happy with my business and art and I've achieved way more than I ever imagined was possible, I still work to improve every single day.

Where is your time best spent?

When creating your schedule the one thing that needs the most of your time is to create the art you love. Make your creation time **SACRED**. No phone calls, no interruptions. Most artists work from home and sometimes it's difficult for others in our life to understand that creating is our job and when we're creating, we're at work and we should not be disturbed while we're at work. If this is the case with you **SET BOUNDARIES**.

Make it a rule that while you are creating that you are not to be interrupted, not unless there's a fire! For you to create your best work you need to harness the energy which is known as flow. Flow is a state of complete and utter concentration and focus, everything else goes away, as if you're in a dreamlike state during your creation process. It's pure and blissful and it's where your masterpieces come from, and every phone alarm or knock on your studio door will take that away from you. Be kind, but absolutely firm about keeping your creation time sacred.

Time wasters

Scrolling through hilarious videos on TikTok is one of my favorite things to do but I get going and laughing and next thing I know it's two days later and I can't remember if I've showered or eaten! Social media is an amazing tool and has allowed me to grow my business and get seen by millions of people all around the globe but if it's not respected it will suck hours out of your day and you will lose valuable time that you can never get back. If you enjoy social media and love to scroll through memes and videos schedule it as a reward and stick to your schedule.

Filter your actions through your vision. When you sit down to watch TV or go to the bar for some drinks ask yourself if it is moving you closer to or further away from your vision.

I'm not suggesting you don't watch TV or take time to go out drinking, what I'm suggesting is that if you choose to do those things, do them with the awareness that you may not be moving closer to your vision as quickly as you would like to.

No time for negativity

Negativity is a time waster. Negativity sucks our will to live and limits our thinking. Just as we create art, we create our lives. Instead of creating with paint or metal or words, our lives are created by what we believe to be true about ourselves. **AGAIN THAT'S WHAT WE <u>BELIEVE</u> TO BE TRUE, NOT WHAT IS <u>ACTUALLY TRUE</u>.** If we believe that we are not worthy of being extremely successful artists, then we will never be able to make it happen no matter how bad we want it.

I'm not suggesting that you blow smoke up your ass with affirmations that you know aren't true, your body knows they are lies. What I am suggestion is that you create a new identity for yourself. Think about a time when you solved a problem, no matter how small the problem was focus on it and remember solving it, remember how it felt solving it. Guess what you are? You're a problem solver! If you can solve that problem, then you can solve other problems and that means any challenge that comes into your life you will figure out!

Why? Because **you're a problem solver and everything is figureoutable!** See, you now have a new identity! ***You're a problem solver!*** It's what you do, it's who you are!

From now on, every time you are faced with a challenge, every time you hear that negativity in your head saying you don't deserve to be an extremely successful artist remind yourself that you are a problem solver and you will figure it out no matter how long it takes.

Time is money

Look at where you spend your time each day and identify anything that you feel is a time waster. If the hour it takes you to get through the grocery store is obnoxious, order groceries online and pick them up in front of the store or have them delivered to your house. If you are charging $100 an hour as an artist doesn't it make much more sense to spend the $5 on delivery fee and spend that hour creating art? What are some other areas you can identify? Mowing the lawn, picking kids up at school, doing the dishes are all menial chores that can be outsourced. Shit, if you have kids make them do the dishes! If you enjoy grocery shopping or washing dishes, then do it! Identifying the time wasters is about finding stuff you don't look forward to and outsourcing them. If you feel that you can't afford someone to come in and do dishes, ask yourself "how can I afford it?"

Time to give back

My greatest feeling as an artist comes when I give back through my art. I've helped people in my community and throughout the country by donating sculptures to charitable auctions, fundraisers, and benefits. I've sent videos to correctional facilities encouraging the inmates to continue to weld and create, donated books, and I've spoken at schools and welding events. Find a cause you believe in and give back whether its speaking or with your art. It's a great way to honor and serve others and it feels really great too!

Patience

In addition to coming out of the womb screaming FREEDOM! I also was born without any patience. When I first went full time as an artist, I expected immediate results. Holy shit was I disappointed! Being an artrepreneur has taught me patience and it is a learnable skill, and if I can learn it anyone can!

Building yourself up to an extremely successful artist is going to take time. How much time? That depends solely on you. The more disciplined you are, the more you study self-improvement, the more deep work you do on the things that matter, the quicker you will get to live inside your vision.

With that being said please don't be in a hurry! Your journey, the challenges you overcome, the experiences you get, the gorgeous art you create will all become part of your story. Embrace every moment, take it all in, revel in it, find joy in your failures and successes! Deeply enjoy every moment, for you will never experience these moments again, and, if you do your job right, they will all be written about in your biography some day!

Your value

When I first started creating art, I didn't understand my value as an artist. I grew up with a "we can't afford that" "money don't grow on trees" "stick those seven slivers of soap together and it will make a whole new bar of soap" mentality. Those beliefs are wonderful for those who wish to be frugal and save money, but they do not serve an artist. For several years I was pricing my art based on how much you would pay for a similar item in a store. For example, I made a toilet paper holder out of horseshoes and saw that toilet paper holders at Walmart were selling for $10 so I priced mine at $15. It sold quickly and I was thrilled but what I didn't understand at the time was that the toilet paper holder was handmade with love and one of a kind, and the one for $10 at Walmart was stamped out in a factory, no love involved, and made for profit. I also didn't see that the time I spent creating that toilet paper holder was time I could never get back.

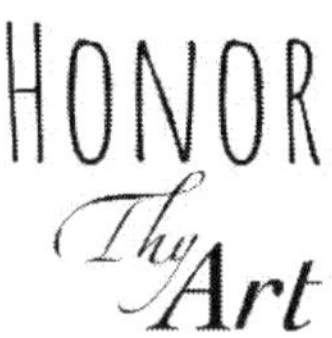

When you create art you're creating with love, and whatever you're creating, it's one of a kind, which means it's valuable. How valuable is it? That all depends on the individual artist. The bigger you grow yourself as an artist the more valuable you become, that's why one artist will earn $100 for a painting and another will earn $1,000,000. Want a bigger paycheck? Grow yourself into an artist who creates $1,000,000 works of art!

Is this possible? Absofreakinglutely! If someone before you has figured out how to create a $1,000,000 work of art so can you! You're a problem solver and this is just another problem you are going to solve! No worries! How do you do it? It's simple but it may not be easy if you had a mentality like mine!!

It took me 5 years to wrap my brain around how valuable my sculptures were! You're welcome to all my clients who bought sculptures in my first 5 years, you are going to see a massive return on investment if you're a collector who buys and sells!

I create my sculptures using scrap metal and because I knew I was using $1.50 worth of scrap metal in a sculpture I had a hard time putting a $1,000 price tag on it. I actually felt guilty for it!

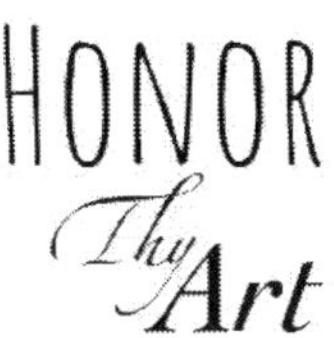

What I know today is my clients didn't see scrap metal, they saw the thousands of hours I poured into honing my craft, improving my skills, and perfecting my art. They were paying for one of a kind art they couldn't get anywhere else, **they were paying for me**!

Art is subjective, meaning one person will look at a work of art and say it's shit, and another person will look at the same work of art and say it's a masterpiece and should be preserved in a museum and guarded at all times.

At the end of the day only you can put the price tag on what you're creating so make sure you are honoring your time by valuing what you are creating! You are truly one of a kind and so is your art! The bigger you grow yourself as an artist the more you can command for your art.

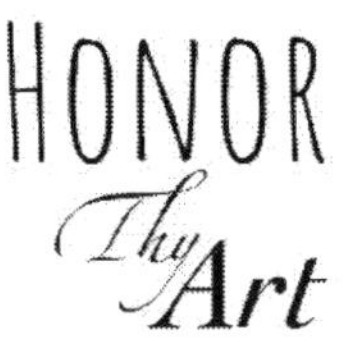

Honor Craft

I stand on the shoulders of skilled welders and fabricators who blessed me with their time and knowledge.

-Barbie The Welder

Craftsmanship is everything and we are only as good as our last work of art. We cannot ride on a success we had two years ago. Honor those who came before you and pave the way for future generations by holding yourself to the highest standards each and every time you create.

When you improve yourself in one area it ends up improving other areas of your life. Schedule time for self-improvement every day. Read, listen to podcasts, watch videos, attend seminars and workshops to grow yourself into a better person. Even if you can only afford 15 minutes a day to improve yourself that adds up to 91.25 hours of self-improvement a year.

It is not merely your job to create as an artist but to push the boundaries of what people think your craft is or can be. Learn from artists in different disciplines and use those techniques to enhance your art.

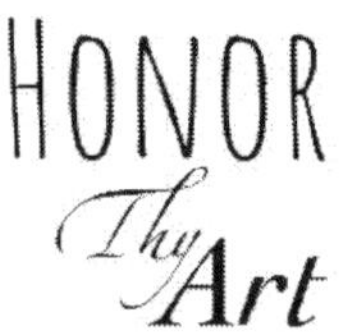

As a welder you would think that I would have nothing to learn from a chainsaw sculptor but in watching them create I saw a technique called relief carving that I later used in my sculpting and created my most exquisite sculpture to date. You never know what technique will forever change the face of your business. When you learn from artists in several different disciplines it will allow you to bring a style that is uniquely you and potentially create a new style or technique that will be part of art history.

Honor education and share your passion and skills with all those who wish to learn. Teaching will bring you a sense of joy you never imagined and allow you to shape the next generation of artists. Teachers are seen as experts in their field. When you teach you're seen as an authority on the subject, as an influencer, someone who shapes the future. You can teach through speaking engagements, writing books, creating how to videos, writing blogs, or simply by holding classes. Don't know how to write a book? Google that shit like I did when I was approached to write my first book. No, really, I Googled how to write a book. You don't have a publisher you say? No problem! Self-publish! Again anything that you don't know how to do, figure it out! You're a creative problem solver! It's what you do!

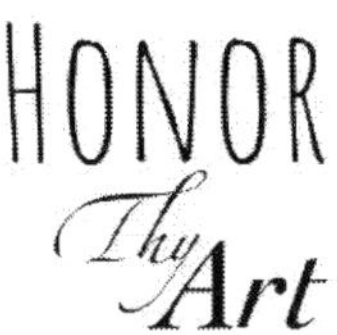

Actively be a champion for your industry, you will honor all the other artists in your industry by doing so, and it's an easy way to be seen as an influencer in your field, someone to look up to. Find non-profits, foundations, and businesses who are championing your industry and work with them. Synergy is powerful and you can both leverage each other's social media and resources, a total win win!

Whether we are painters, singers, cake makers, graphic designers, or sculptors honoring our craft is what we do, it's who we are!

Honor Brand

Brand is legacy.

-Barbie The Welder

If you search "how to brand a business", you get all kinds of information that I feel is wrong for artists. What works for major corporations I don't feel works well for artists. **As an artist *you* are your brand.** Think about Bob Ross and what image comes to mind? That sexy ass afro of his! You can recognize that man a mile away! Did he do this on purpose? Who knows, but it's possible that he is one of the most easily recognizable artists in the modern world! Bob was known for his love of animals, that great hair style, and his incredible ability to make anyone feel like they could create masterful works of art as he soothingly encouraged you to paint happy little trees. Bob made creating works of art accessible to anyone and made you feel good about what you were creating! Bob isn't around anymore but his image can be seen in memes, on shirts, coffee mugs, toys, and all kinds of swag.

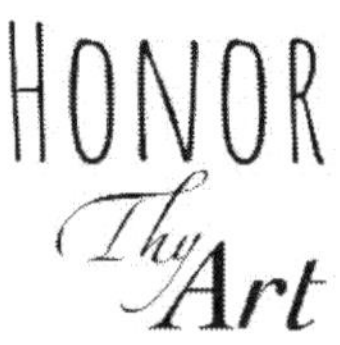

The proper branding of an individual will create legacy that will live on long after we're gone. That's what branding did for Bob Ross and it's what it will do for you if you work at it! If you haven't seen The Joy of Painting with Bob Ross that's your homework. Episodes are on YouTube for free!

Creating your brand

Your brand is how you stand out in a crowd and should be one of your finest masterpieces! Branding yourself really just means embracing your values, being true to who you are, owning your badassery and then consistently showing that to the world.

Do not rush creating your brand, it will develop over time. As you are working to create your brand study famous individuals and see how they have branded themselves. Study famous chefs, queens, basketball players, speakers, and icons as well as famous artists, this will allow you to see a wide variety of individual branding techniques and come up with a brand that is truly unique. Learn from these people but stay true to who you are otherwise you will come across as a fraud, and no one likes a fraud.

Your brand has several layers like a yummy cake. How you look/act is part of your brand, and so is a logo, and finally the style in which you create is also part of your brand.

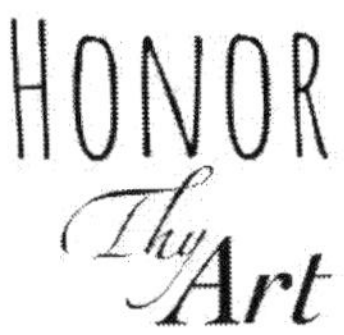

Branding, not just for cows

When branding yourself areas to look at are

Clothes you wear (Style, color, brand) or maybe you don't wear clothes!

How your hair is styled or colored or cut

How you talk or certain words you use

How you walk

The colors you use in your logo and or pictures

Quirks you have

Being humble, flashy, or loud

Are you inspirational or a wild child or an inspirational wild child!

How you teach if you choose to do so

Props you always carry like a hat, cane, sunglasses, jacket, or funky shoes

Brand yourself from head to toe but please brand yourself based on your values and not the values of others.

BE TRUE TO YOU! Not everyone is going to like you, but then again not everyone has good taste!

Your logo

You will need a logo that will be used in all of your marketing. Your logo can be a picture, symbol, letter(s,) number(s), your signature, or any combination of those. It needs to represent you and your business. When you are creating your logo stay true to yourself, if you are goofy and love being goofy then create a goofy logo.

All great logos are easily recognizable. They are consistent in colors, shape, and font. When designing your logo consider colors you love or resonate with, a font you find appealing, and shapes or designs that make you happy.

Your logo will be used in your marketing, on products, apparel, and swag so please keep in mind that if you desire both men and women to wear your branded merchandise that your logo should be true to you but still appealing to both men and women.

Every artist will approach creating a logo in their own unique way. Whether you create your logo or hire another artist to create it this is something to play with and have fun doing!

If you hire someone to create your logo make sure that you will own the rights to that logo and pay extra for that right if you need to, but you MUST own the rights for your logo.

Once you have your logo it should go on EVERY SINGLE PICTURE you post on social media. My suggestion is until you get your logo use a consistent font and write your name on all the pictures you post. Branding your pictures will protect your property and hard work. It's a shitass thing to do but on occasion someone may take pictures that don't belong to them and use them to sell their products. When your name or logo is on your pictures at the very least people can find you if they choose.

Brand your art

Part of your brand will be the style of art you create. Unless you are very lucky, in the beginning of your career you may have to create all kinds of stuff just so that you can pay the bills and keep creating and improving your art, but always be aiming for your niche, the subject that you want to create exclusively. Every chance you get, make the art that makes your heart sing, and get down to one subject as soon as you possible can. Mastering one subject will allow you to develop raving fans, people who are absolutely devoted to you because everything you create speaks to them.

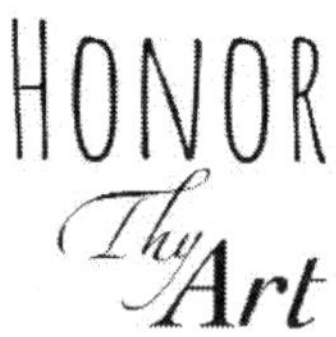

Raving fans will buy whatever you create, wait for every video you put out, watch the whole thing, like, comment and share it with their friends and family, and will wait in line for an hour to get a photograph with you and an autograph!

How will you know you've done a great job branding your business? People will say "WOW!" People will want your art, a shirt with your logo on it, your calendar, and a coffee mug with your mug on it! People will recognize your art, you, or see something that reminds them of you, and they will send you messages telling you so, and most fun of all you will get recognized when you go places and people will want to take pictures with you and tell their friends and social media followers that they met you!

Now let's talk about how we're going to leverage all that branding!

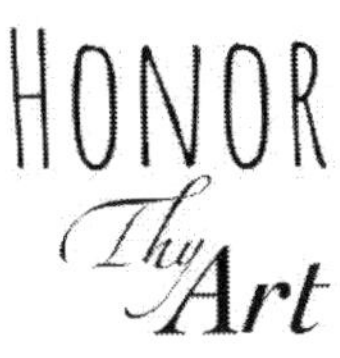

Honor Marketing

Marketing showcases your business, creates hype around your brand, and lets clients know how they can find and work with you.

-Barbie The Welder

Marketing, done correctly, will showcase your art in such a way that you will not have to sell your art, clients will want to buy from you and seek you out to do so.

Content is king and our world is quickly becoming completely digital. The businesses with the most online content will get the most attention! Think about your behavior. How do you find a business? How do you shop? How much time do you spend on social media? How do you learn new things? The answer for most people is online!

Showcase your business

A picture is worth a thousand words, but if you can't tell what the picture is the first five words will be, "what the hell is that?"

If you don't already have the skill of **excellent** photography and videography and you can't afford or barter with an amazing photographer/videographer, **it is of utmost importance that you spend time every day, (schedule it) learning how to take excellent pictures and videos.** No matter what kind of art you are involved in you need to produce excellent visual content for your marketing.

You don't need fancy equipment to produce excellent photography/videography, (here on out referred to as content) I have been using my cell phone, tripod, and a couple apps, most free and some I've paid for, to create all my content. What you need are the skills to use what equipment you have and be able to edit what you capture so that it resonates with your audience. If your cell phone or camera isn't able to take quality videos or pictures your next investment needs to be something that will. **IMMEDIATELY** if not sooner!

How do you know what to take pictures or videos of? Find some artists you love to watch online and see what they are doing! In fact, study a bunch of them! You can then research how to do it if you can't figure it out! In the beginning you might copy people, but what you need to work towards is developing your own style for how you are showcasing yourself, your art, and your process, this will also be part of your brand.

You need to be a thought leader, an influencer, the one everyone else looks to for inspiration! Don't freak out! Like all things this will develop over time with patience and practice!

I want you to try a whole bunch of different techniques and styles and see what works and feels right to you and do a whole lot of that!

Create hype around your brand

Most companies have an entire department dedicated to marketing and a budget to run that department. My guess is that you have neither the department nor budget! Social media = FREE marketing and advertising, which means it's free to reach clients all over the world and let them know about you, your art, and your products.

If you are not tech savvy then schedule time to study every single day until you are and then do at least a monthly refresher on the newest social media marketing trends. I study through people I find on YouTube who have dedicated their lives to teaching marketing. Not every person's teaching will resonate with you so keep looking until you find someone who does. If you don't like learning through videos then listen to podcasts, read, do whatever it takes to learn and stay current.

Get a schedule and stick to it as best you can, but only post quality content. If it takes you a week to get quality content, then so be it, but work your ass off to get quality content and make it a goal to post once a day. How do you know your content is quality content? You will get feedback each time you post to social media. Post something and then see if you get likes, comments, and shares. Some of your content will do better than others. Study what is doing well and do more of that. Time of day, content, hashtags, platform all play into how well a post will do. Play around and problem solve until you find what works for you.

Each social media platform may have a different time of day that your posts will get better engagement. (If you don't know what engagement is on social media study it and then track it as you are posting to help you see what is working and what is not) Instagram posts might do better at 6 pm and LinkedIn posts might do better at 6am. This will be trial and error for you. What works for one person may not for another. Just work at it every day until you find a schedule that works for you and then stick to it. Posting at consistent times on each platform will allow your supporters to know they can count on you and that will help build brand loyalty.

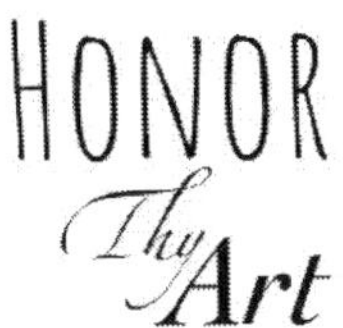

Social media is about being SOCIAL, not just posting shit, getting likes and leaving! The people I admire the most on social media are the ones who take time for their supporters, no matter how large their following is. The larger your following grows the more challenging this will become but you are a problem solver so I know you will figure this out. I deeply suggest (READ: DO IT) that you schedule time each day to respond to any comments or messages you receive on social media. A simple thumbs up or smiley face emoji works to let someone know you read their comment but responding with a "thank you Bill" will really show your supporters you are grateful they took their valuable time to look at what you are doing. Again social media is about being social and if someone in person complimented your work you sure as shit better not ignore them! I love when someone writes to me and I respond, and then I get a message back saying how amazed people are that I responded! It's all about honoring and respecting those who support you. The more you honor them the more they will respect you. Look, there are millions of people out there online they could be watching, and they chose you. Give them all the love and respect that you are capable of.

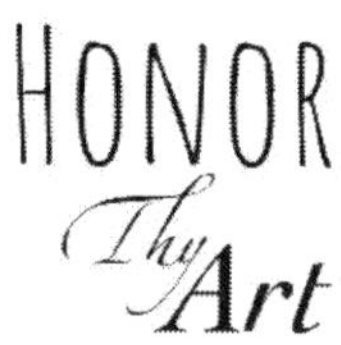

What should you be posting? Again each platform will dictate ultimately the content you post but for the most part people want you, your art, and your process of creation. Unless your art is food do not post your meals people! Most people don't give a flying rat shit about what you're eating, your vacation, or the new car you bought. Keep your page strictly business, you, your art, your studio, your process, your branded merchandise, YOU! Do not make your supporters wade through a pile of shit to get to your art! With that being said, let me throw you a curveball. As your following grows and you become a world renowned artist your followers might want to see more of your life. If that's the case, then give them what they want as long as it's in alignment with your values and vision.

All social media is not treated equal so which platforms are right for you? That will depend totally on you. Study each platform and see which ones will suit your needs. If I had to make a recommendation for the platforms I feel are musts I would say Instagram, YouTube, LinkedIn and Twitter. Why? A large Instagram following will allow you to showcase your art and work with companies as an influencer, YouTube will allow you to teach and market your business, LinkedIn will allow you to inspire and get clients, and Twitter will allow you to be quoted.

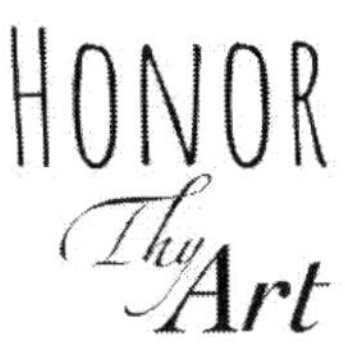

Every artist is different, and a platform that works for one might not work for another, but by all means get on a variety of platforms, study each one and see what works on each, and then stay consistent with posting quality content.

Treat social media the same way you would treat someone you just met. You wouldn't walk up to someone you just met and say buy my art. You want to add value to a person's life, ask about them, get to know them, and then, only if they ask, will you tell them about you.

How do you do that? Post content with a relevant quote from you or quote someone else or ask a question to get a conversation started, then add your website or a link to a video you've created. This will add value while giving people a way to seek you out if they so choose.

Your audience will dictate to you what they like to see. Stay true to yourself but give them what they want. Experiment with what posts gets good traction, likes, comments, and shares. Track your analytics, continue to educate yourself about each platform you are on, and be patient with yourself, even pages with millions of followers started at zero. Like all things in business this is long game, it will take time.

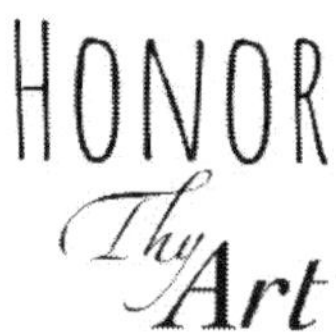

Every business needs a website, and yours is no different. If you can't afford to have one created for your, bartering is a great way to get stuff you can't afford, or study and learn how to make a beautiful website and make it yourself.

Your website needs to showcase your art, feature your branding, let clients know how they can reach you, and guide people to all of your social media. Keep your website clean and easy to navigate. Again this is something that you will work at and refine over time.

Your business will need business cards. Your business card needs to clearly identify who you are, what you specialize in, and how the bearer can contact you. If your art is visual I suggest a high quality picture of your art or you with your art on the back of your business card, a picture is worth a thousand words.

Rogue Marketing is my hands down, favorite way to market. I'm an artist and I love being creative and rogue marketing allows me to do that. Rogue marketing is marketing in a way that a traditional business would not think to advertise. For example, any business can slap a sign on the side of their vehicle but when you're a metal sculptor you can create a piece of art that goes on your vehicle and whenever you travel people will see exactly what you can do.

My 6 foot tall sculpture of Jack Skellington holding a sign with my name on it in one hand and pointing to it with the other hand riding around in the back of my truck had a whole lot of people taking pictures and sending them to me through my social media. GO ROGUE and think up creative ways to showcase your skills and let people know you exist.

Pay for a custom license plate, paint your car if you're a painter or someone who can draw, just think outside of the box!

However you choose to do your marketing you need to have a clear and consistent message across everything you do.

Let clients know how they can find and work with you

Your marketing needs to include information so your clients to know how to easily contact you and how they can work with you. Your social media biographies need to have your website and link to your other social media, every video posted to YouTube should have your website listed in it, and your website should have your social media linked to it. Your website should have a way for potential clients to contact you, and how they can have a custom piece created, or they can commission you to write a song, bake a cake, or do whatever it is that you do!

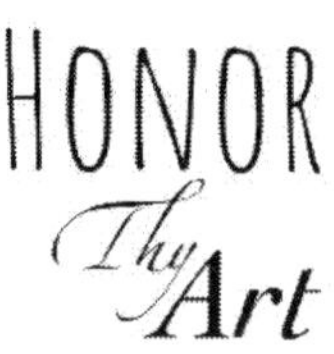

Don't make it hard for clients to give you money! Make the process to contact you and commission art or hire your services as easy as possible.

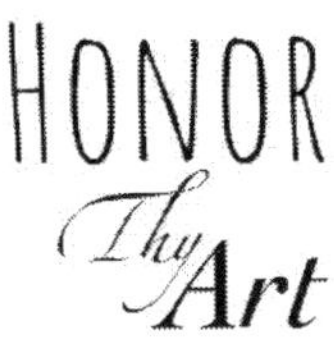

Honor Clients

People say do what you love, and you'll never work a day in your life but that's untrue. When you do what you love you work twice as hard because you're passionate about what you're working on and you're working for YOU Incorporated!

-Barbie The Welder

Knowing who your ideal client is and finding them will lead to extreme happiness and success as an artist. Your ideal client may change over the course of your career but the process of finding and serving them will remain a constant.

It is time to go on an ideal client treasure hunt. Your ideal client will depend on what you are creating. A singer may be looking for a totally different client than a painter. To find your ideal client consider what you are creating and who would want to buy it. Do you create large paintings? Would hotel owners want to buy them? Where do hotel owners hang out? Are hotel owners the decision makers when it comes to buying art? Is there a person who buys art for hotels? Are you creating caricatures? Would your ideal client be people traveling on vacation and is there a place you could position yourself where it would be very easy for them to find you?

If you are not creating exactly what you want at the moment who would want to buy the art that you really want to create? How can you position yourself as an artist who wants to create that type of art so that you can attract those buyers to you?

As an example: Although I was selling my simple sculptures and my mass produced art to middle class women at craft shows and events, I found that men who owned businesses were the primary buyers of my masterpieces. More than anything I wanted to create the masterpieces, so I went on a treasure hunt to find where male business owners were. Guess what I found? LinkedIn was a hotbed of male businessowners! (Does that sound sexual to you?) I started to grow my LinkedIn network and studied what people on LinkedIn responded to best and geared my marketing towards that, and then JACKPOT, I found treasure!

I've never liked the word sell. Selling has negativity around it and makes me think of the greasy car salesman who talked me into buying the 1982 VW Rabbit POS I got when I was 19. I hate being sold to, but I do, however, love to buy things. I buy things all the time and no one has to talk me into it. Chances are you feel the same way, and so does your client.

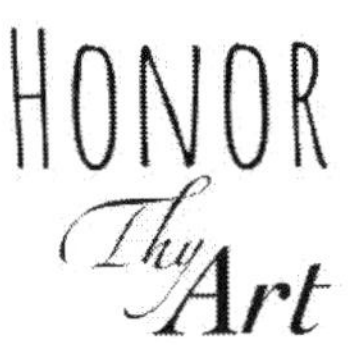

Repeat after me: **I WILL NOT BE A GREASY CAR SALESPERSON!**

We are not salespeople; we are providers of service and value. Our goal is to create so much value around our art that clients flock to us and want to buy it. How do you create value around you and your art? Create the most amazing art you are capable of, take the most amazing pictures/videos of what you are creating, showcase it on social media with your exquisite marketing skills, when people comment on your posts you respond to each and every person with a positive comment, and when you have clients you treat them with honor and respect and you give them more value then they expect to receive. Easy, peasy, lemon squeezy.

Chances are at some point during your career you may end up with a client who is less than savory. The client may be demanding, rude, controlling, or disrespectful. Here you will face a choice only you can make, work with them knowing they will be difficult, or choose to not to work with them. If you choose to work with someone who is less than ideal, you made the choice so please treat them with the same love and respect that you would treat a dream client. Choose to be all in 100% or don't get in at all. In the past when my business was new, I had to work with everyone and anyone. If someone was rude, disrespectful, or demanding I charged a premium I lovingly refer to as

Dickhead Fee. (This does NOT go on the invoice!) I doubled what I would normally charge, that way if they agreed to work with me, I was super excited to work with them knowing it would be worth it. Today I choose to only work with ideal clients.

Your goal is to grow yourself as an artist to be so financially stable that you can pick and choose the clients you work with so that you are radically excited to work on every single project.

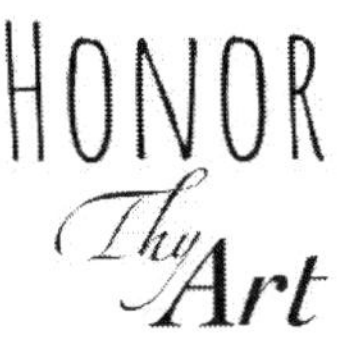

Honor Sponsorship

Finding and working with companies that are in alignment with your artistry and mission is a total win win.

-Barbie The Welder

If your friend, someone you trusted, said I used this deodorant and I love it, wouldn't you be more apt to try it than if a total stranger told you about it? Marketing has drastically changed over the last few years. Today, companies are actively seeking influencers, (people who have large social media following) to tell their supports to use a company's product. You don't need to have a huge following to get free products, having the attention of a couple thousand people can really help a company sell products! Want free products and an income? Growing a large social media following will not only allow you to market your art, you can potentially get free products, a stream of income, and be able to leverage that companies social media following!

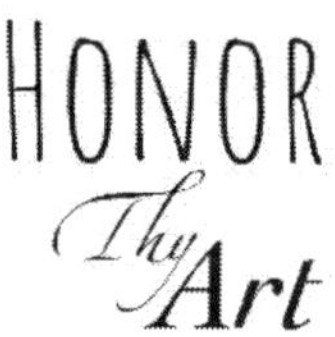

As your social media grows you will have companies reach out to you and offer you product and money. **Only work with companies you would feel comfortable putting your reputation on the line for** because that is what you do every time you post a picture of you with a product. You worked your ass off to get where you are, and no amount of money or product is worth losing it. Reputation is everything!

Early in my career I was faced with a decision to work with a company I didn't believe in for a lot of money, that I desperately needed, or refuse the offer and possibly not be able to pay my bills. I refused the offer and struggled to pay my bills but felt great that I honored my values. That company's reputation would have affected mine. That deal, even thought I would have been better off financially, could have damaged my credibility and lost me my business.

So how do you get the attention of multimillion dollar companies? You give to get. What kind of products do you use in your art? Are you fond of a certain camera, paintbrush, microphone, crayons? Showcase those products in your pictures and videos and tag the companies when you post. You can check their social media page and see if they have specific hashtags they prefer, most of them will tell you right in their bio what hashtag to use for them share your picture on their page.

Get their attention enough and they will reach out to you and offer free product or even better money to work with them.

When a company reaches out to you, you have more power than if you go knocking at their door. They want to work with you which gives you the leverage. Ask them what their proposal is and don't be afraid to make a counteroffer. Make sure the compensation you will receive is worth your time.

If a company shares your content on their page a couple times and you don't hear from them reach out to them and ask about working together. The larger your social media following the more valuable you are to them so keep that in mind when working out a deal. You will be helping them sell product and so make sure the deal is worth your time. Scared to ask to work with a company? Do you have a paid sponsorship right now? No? Well then you have nothing to lose and everything to gain!

Chances are you're not going to get paid right away. What a company will need to see is value over time, so that's what you need to give them. They won't offer you thousands of dollars for two or three good posts. Building your reputation as a loyal consumer and promoter of their product will take time.

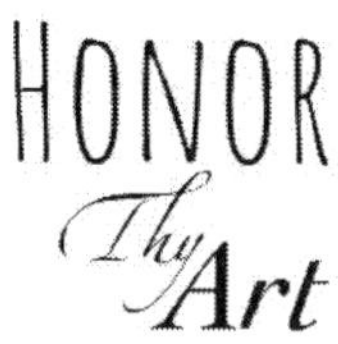

When you work with a company not only should you get free merch and possibly paid you also get to leverage their social media and clients. Even if it's not helping you sell more art it allows you to grow your social media which makes you more valuable!

Don't be a product whore. Need I say more?

Honor Dream Chasers

Find and connect with people who are chasing their dream, for they are powerful and uplifting and will show you that anything is possible!

-Barbie The Welder

You have this huge vision that you've created for yourself, you can picture it just as clear as day, and you know damn well that you are going to make this vision a reality, but most people are not going to be able to see it. Not only will they not be able to see it but some of them will actually try to talk you out of it based on their own need for security, small thinking, lack of imagination, or dismal work ethic. If you have dream stealers in your life avoid them like the plague if at all possible or just don't talk to them about your huge vision, talk to them about the weather, they like that.

Find and connect with likeminded individuals. When you are thinking and dreaming huge it is super important to be around as many huge thinkers as you possibly can so you can support each other's dreams! To find huge thinkers locally look for entrepreneur groups. Find and attend these groups and connect with people who are out there living their dream.

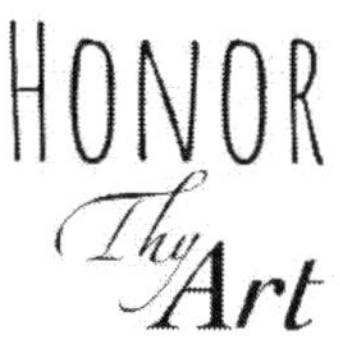

One of the best things I did for my business in the beginning was to join a local entrepreneur group. At first I didn't understand what they were talking about, business matters were foreign to me, but I continued to attend because it was nice to get out of my shop for a bit and connect with other humans. The longer I attended the meetings the more I began to understand and the stronger my business grew. I would bring my current business card in and pass them around and ask the group how I could improve it. I had them give me feedback on several areas of my business and I took their advice and quickly made changes to improve my business. I found another local artist and became best friends with them. Later in another entrepreneur group I found three artists who invited me to their accountability group where once a month we share our goals with each other and encourage each other.

Many of the entrepreneurs that attended the meetings were local businesses who were thinking locally but over time my vision was to build a global brand, I wanted to find and connect with entrepreneurs who were thinking globally. I first found those entrepreneurs in books and through social media. I read everything they wrote, watched every video, and took their advice and soon I was seeing results.

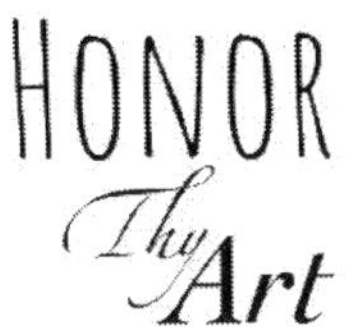

I had the absolute privilege of spending a month with Bogi Lateiner, a deeply inspirational entrepreneur who gave me the advice that to take myself to the next level I should attend self-improvement seminars and get a mentor. That's exactly what I did slightly before I could afford it. What I learned from those seminars and the mentor allowed me to take my business and art to insane levels that I would have never imagined possible and I got way more value than I expected! The seminars were lifechanging! I learned that I was much stronger mentally then I ever imagined, I connected with the most incredible huge thinkers who were super supportive of my vision and encouraged me to think even bigger than I was!

Not every entrepreneur group may be right for you, not every self-improvement video may be right for you, and not every book will be right for you. It's your mission to find the ones that are right for you and soak up as much knowledge as you possibly can! Schedule time every day to learn from dream chasers! You are too big to think or play small.

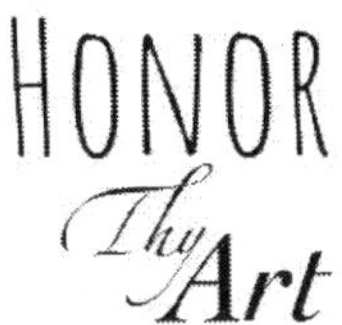

Honor Financial Intelligence

Passive income equals freedom.

-Barbie The Welder

You can sell three huge commissions, or a song, or a video, make a big ass profit and then see nothing but tumbleweeds for the next 7 months. There is no rhyme or reason when it comes to selling art, no consistency, therefore your financial discipline is super important.

Financial discipline

My system for financial discipline is that I have four bank accounts, one for bills that 50% of any income goes into, one for savings that 20% of any income goes into, one for my dream shop that 20% of any income goes into and one for travel that 10% of any income goes into. When money goes into the account it does not come out unless it is to be used for what it has been earmarked for. If I owe bills and don't have the money in my bills account, then the bill does not get paid, I won't pull money from my savings to pay a bill. Is it scary to not pay a bill? For me yes so it gets my creative ass in overdrive figuring out what I can do to earn the money for the bills.

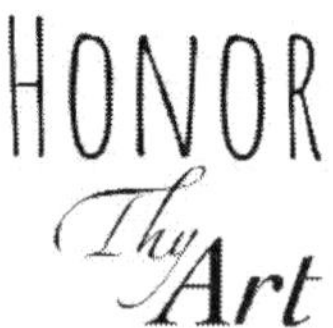

In the beginning of my career I sold a lot of my toys to afford to continue as an artist full time. It was hard to watch my motorcycle and boats go bye bye, so very early in my career I learned to be disciplined behind my money making sure to only buy what was necessary, keeping my bills as low as possible, not overextending myself when I did make money, and to save for a rainy day.

This system works for me and has kept me in a very good place financially, but each person has different financial needs. Look at the areas you need to fund, create accounts for them, choose what percentage of your income will go into each account and then stay disciplined.

I reinvest every penny of my money into my business and in the 5.5 years I've been a full time artist I have yet to take a paycheck. I pay my bills, buy what food I need, buy clothing when necessary, I pay for my education, but the bulk of my money has gone directly back into my business. I buy lighting, better equipment, material, tools or whatever is needed to allow me to create better sculptures. Over time this has allowed me to build a very strong business foundation. Great sacrifice great reward and I know it won't be like this forever. By being disciplined now it will allow me to do amazing things later. Remember the long game!

Passive income

What has allowed me the freedom to create what I want when I want and be very picky about who I take on as a client? Multiple streams of passive income around my discipline.

If your goal is to create what you absolutely love, when you want to create it and for whom you want to create it then passive income is the answer you've been looking for. Passive income is income you get when you create something once and then get paid over and over again without having to do any more work. Its name is kind of deceiving because you do have to do the work first, but then PAYDIRT!!! An example of passive income is this book. I am writing it, putting in the work, will publish it, market it, and then you will buy it from a retailer who will deliver it to you and then they will deposit money in my bank account once a month. Once the book is finished, I will get paid each month until I die in which case my kids will start getting the money, and then if they have kids their kids will get the money when they die. Work once, get paid again and again.

Books are brilliant streams of passive income, but they are not the only way! Once you build up your YouTube channel, or other video channel, you can monetize your account.

When you have a monetized account you get paid for the minutes people watch your videos and then get a deposit in your bank account each month. The more minutes your videos are watched the more money you will make. Make the videos once, get paid again and again.

Affiliate marketing is another way to make passive income. When you are using products you love in your creation you can use affiliate links to the products and get paid if someone purchases those products using your links. I use the Amazon affiliate program and when someone asks me what welder I'm using I send them my affiliate link to the welder on Amazon, if they buy the welder, I get a percentage of the total sale. I will not promote something that I don't 100% stand behind and respect as a brand and I suggest you do the same. Again, reputation is everything!

Branded merchandise

Are you ready to create some great hype around your brand and make passive income? Branded merchandise will help bring awareness to you and your art, allow your supporters to support you, and can bring you a glorious stream of passive income!

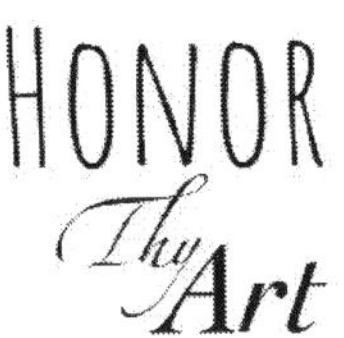

Find and use companies where you can upload your logo onto merchandise, they print it and send it and then send you the profit. If you have quotes or saying that people associate with you put those on shirts, mugs, keychains, and other swag. If you're painting or drawing or sculpting your supporters might not be able to afford one of your original works of art but having a high quality image on a mug, poster, or shirt might be something they can't live without!

Are you writing poetry or songs? Put your popular lyrics on a shirt or mug! Think of all the possibilities to create merchandise with your art!

Create your own product line. You heard me correctly! Product lines are not just for major corporations! Are you a painter? How badass would it be to have your own line of paintbrushes! Oh, it's a thing! How about a musician who loves whisky or wine? Get together with a local distillery or winery and play let's make a deal! A couple years back I had an idea for a product line of metal art welding kits, essentially 3D metal puzzles aspiring welders or sculptors could quickly and easily create and feel successful! I had never created a product, let alone a product line, and I had never programmed or run a CNC machine before. Am I a problem solver? You betcha! Did I invest my savings into a $12,000 machine I never programmed or ran before? Shore nuf! Did I figure out how to program it?

Absofreakinglutely! Do I now have a product line of 5 metal art welding kits that have sold in 4 different countries and are selling in a retail location? Damn straight! Is that a stream of income passive? Not yet! Will I eventually problem solve how to make it completely passive? You can bet on it! Why? Because I'm a creative problem solver and everything is figureoutable!

Passive income has been the answer to my creative freedom but there are so many other ways. It is your responsibility to study financial literacy and learn as much as you can about money. It's crazy that it's such a taboo subject with so many people. You will quickly learn that people who are financially literate will talk about their net worth and those who are not will talk about their debt. What does that tell you? Schedule time to study money at least once a week and more often if you can! Find the people out there talking about money and finance that resonates with you and learn everything you can.

Like the entrepreneur meetings, when I first studied money, I was freakin lost, but like the entrepreneur meeting I stuck in there and keep listening and learning and eventually it started making sense.

The average millionaire has 7 streams of passive income, I have 11 streams and my goal is 13 because I love to think HUGE!

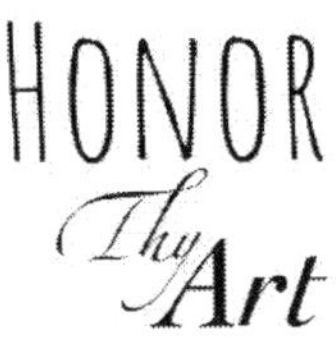

Honor Relevance

Reinventing myself and my business has allowed me to not only stay relevant but be the driving force in new trends.

-Barbie The Welder

As you work on growing yourself, improving your art, and creating a fantastic business foundation, your vision will grow. When I first went full time as an artist I was traveling to shows and events every week. At that time I believed that was the only way make money as an artist, so I worked to perfect my business. I worked to improve my packing so it would be easier to get my art to the events, I improved my booth set up, and I started researching shows to see which were the best, and I only attended the ones that would have a great turnout. One day, I was set up at my local fair and I was frustrated. I was upset because I had to sit on my ass in that booth for 72 hours during that week and not be in my shop creating. I was also upset because I had been mass producing art and other than improving how long it took me to create 40 Big Dick Hot Dog Cookers (Yeah, that was a product, there's a YouTube video!) my skills were not improving.

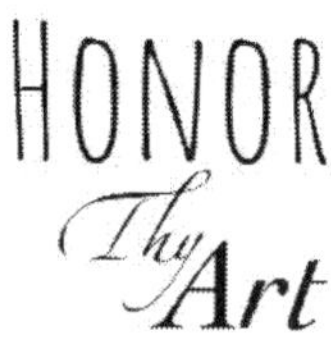

Reinvent yourself

I decided that although I was finally able to comfortably feed my belly, traveling to these shows every week (48 shows in 52 weeks in 2015) and mass producing art wasn't feeding my soul. I wasn't making the one of a kind sculptures that really pushed me as an artist and made me happy. It was time to make a change. It was August, and I made up my mind that during the next 4 months I would teach myself how to sell online and only set up and sell at my 3 of favorite shows in 2016. It was a frightening decision because 90% of my income was coming from those shows and only 10% online. It was really important for me to spend as much time creating as possible, so over the next 4 months I poured myself into studying how to grow my social media organically and how to sell online. The first 3 months of 2016 were scary as shit! I was thrilled to have so much time to create my art, but no sales poured in, people were not ordering stuff from my Etsy shop or contacting me to create custom orders. The little savings I had in the bank was disappearing rapidly. I continued to create art every day and at night I would study how to sell online and grow social media, and slowly my hard work started paying off and my online sales and requests for commissions began to increase.

I could have continued to sell at shows every week, I was learning what sold quickly, was making good money and thriving financially, but I wasn't thriving emotionally. The difficult decision I made to reinvent my business not only allowed me to grow as an artist and feed my soul, it also allowed me to grow my business financially and allowed me to be relevant in the welding and art worlds.

Reinvent yourself again

Fast forward to 2017 and not only have I've been happily selling art online and growing my social media for a year and a half, I'd also written my first book. (Nobody saw that coming!) My bank account was full, but again I felt my soul was not. I was spending a majority of my time creating like I had wanted to, but a majority of my income was from massed produced art like my horseshoe wine racks and the Big Dick Hotdog Cookers, not the one of a kind sculptures that really make my heart sing and fed my soul.

Again I made a terrifying decision, that as of 2018 I would only create one of a kind art. Again it was very slow, and the transition took time, but my hard work and dedication to my decision paid off. I poured myself into my one of a kind creations, and when I didn't have a custom order from a client, I just made whatever spoke to my soul. My art improved rapidly, and I was skipping into my shop every day super stoked to be doing what I was doing.

I worked even harder to grow my social media, improve my photography/videography, and clients and business showed up wanting to work with me. I made everything from birds to company logos and my bank account grew!

And again

Creating the one of a kind art was so much fun, and damn was the money great, but again I felt something was off. Some of the sculptures I was creating had me running into the shop but for others I had to force myself to work on them. When I choose to finally look at the situation it was quickly apparent what was happening, the angels, demons, skulls, and surreal creatures really made me happy, but everything else didn't. Again I made the decision to pivot my business and I cut out everything that wasn't in alignment with the things I wanted to create.

Making these big changes was difficult but easy. It's difficult to walk away from a stable stream of income but making the decision to feed my soul resulted in feeding my belly each and every time, and actually resulted in a higher income every single time!

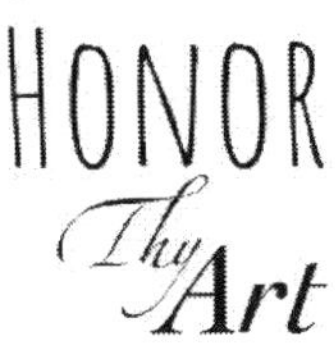

The Cher Factor

As an artist I can't imagine doing anything else for a living, however, what's working for me today will not work for me in 5 years.

Times change and so do people, and in order to thrive financially and emotionally as an artist and stay relevant, I embody something I call The Cher Factor. Cher is someone who has not just survived as an artist over decades but has thrived and is still kicking ass and creating art today! Someone who embodies The Cher Factor is someone who is consistently improving and reinventing themself, creates trends, and stays relevant over decades.

How does someone embody The Cher Factor? They honor themselves and their art today but are always thinking "what's next." They ask themselves questions that keep them thinking about the future. How can I stand out in a crowd? How can I reinvent myself? How can I create my art better or different? Am I resisting change in any area of my life and would it help to embrace it? How can I be seen as an influencer? What could I do to start a new trend? What other artists could I learn from that would add to my art? What could I do that no one else has thought to do? What product line could I create? What is a new strategy to market myself? Who could I collaborate with to put myself in front of a new audience? Do I have any beliefs that are holding me back and what are some new beliefs I could embrace?

Staying relevant is an art, and just like anything that you create it takes time, patience, and practice. Come up with a list of questions you can ask yourself on a regular basis that will keep you thinking toward your future.

Honor Thy Art

As you design and create your art utopia you will have to wear many hats, but your most important hat is your artist hat. Your art feeds your soul, and when you create from love you pour that into the world and now more than ever we need that love, we need your beautiful art!

Although my writing ends here my support will go on FOREVER! Connect with me on my personal social media, @BarbieTheWelder on Instagram and YouTube, and Barbie The Welder on LinkedIn and Facebook.

View the sculptures that fill my heart and soul with love on my website **BarbieTheWelder.com**

Follow us @HonorThyArt and #honorthyart when you post your art on Instagram to get your art featured on our page.

Go to **HonorThyArt.com** for more resources!

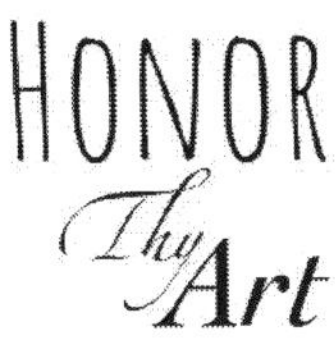

About The Author

My worst day as an artist is still better than my best day working for someone else!

-Barbie The Welder

I took a six month welding program in 2007 after seeing the woman welding giant angel wings in the movie Castaway starring Tom Hanks, the scene just spoke my soul and I immediately knew that I needed to be a metal sculptor. I was hired at a custom fabrication shop in 2008 after I graduated and worked there for 3.5 years before I was able to save enough for a down payment to purchase a home, for the garage. It took me 9 more months of working and saving before I had enough money to purchase the machines and tools I needed for my home studio. I worked in my garage every night after work and every weekend designing and creating anything I could think of. I left the fabricating job I loved a year and a half later to go all in on myself as a full time artist on September 1st, 2014.

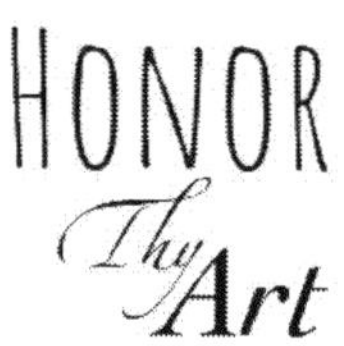

Since that time I have failed my way to success and over the last 5.5 years I've been a full-time artist I've sculpted a life for myself that is beyond my wildest dreams. So far I've had the honor of designing and creating sculptures for major corporations including Miller Welders, Harley-Davidson, Weiler Abrasives, Chicago Pneumatic, and Carolina Shoe Company, and I've worked with small businesses and exclusive clients in 15 different countries. I have welded sculptures live in front of thousands of people at Sturgis Motorcycle Rally, Americade Motorcycle Rally and SEMA in Las Vegas, and I've even presented sculptures to my clients live on stage at the Full Throttle Saloon and at Harley Davidson's 115 anniversary! Each month my YouTube channel draws viewers from more than 50 countries and so far, I've written 5 books!

There's no telling what I'll do next so make sure you stay tuned!

Made in the USA
Middletown, DE
28 May 2020

96124819R00046